Childhoods of the Presidents

James Monroe

Childhoods of the Presidents

John Adams
George W. Bush
Bill Clinton
Ulysses S. Grant
Andrew Jackson
Thomas Jefferson
John F. Kennedy
Abraham Lincoln
James Madison
James Monroe
Ronald Reagan
Franklin D. Roosevelt
Theodore Roosevelt
Harry S. Truman
George Washington
Woodrow Wilson

James Monroe

Hal Marcovitz

Mason Crest Publishers
Philadelphia

RAP 867 2372

Produced by OTTN Publishing, Stockton, New Jersey

Mason Crest Publishers
370 Reed Road
Broomall, PA 19008
www.masoncrest.com

Copyright © 2003 by Mason Crest Publishers. All rights reserved. Printed and bound in the Hashemite Kingdom of Jordan.

First printing

1 3 5 7 9 8 6 4 2

Library of Congress Cataloging-in-Publication Data
Marcovitz, Hal.
    James Monroe / Hal Marcovitz.
      p.   cm.   (Childhood of the presidents)
    Summary: A biography of the fifth president of the United States, focusing on his childhood and young adulthood.
    Includes bibliographical references and index.
      ISBN 1-59084-283-9
    1. Monroe, James, 1758-1831—Childhood and youth—Juvenile literature. 2. Monroe, James, 1758-1831—Juvenile literature. 3. Presidents—United States—Biography—Juvenile literature. [1. Monroe, James, 1758-1831—Childhood and youth. 2. Presidents.] I. Title. II. Series.
E372.M26 2003
973.5'4'092—dc21
[B]   2002069206

Publisher's note: All quotations in this book come from original sources, and contain the spelling and grammatical inconsistencies of the original text.

Childhoods of the Presidents

Table of Contents

Introduction 6
Arthur M. Schlesinger, jr.

Times that Try Men's Souls 9

Westmoreland County 19

William and Mary 27

Williamsburg 31

The Era of Good Feelings 37

Chronology 42

Glossary 43

Further Reading 44

Internet Resources 45

Index 46

★ *Introduction* ★

Alexis de Tocqueville began his great work *Democracy in America* with a discourse on childhood. If we are to understand the prejudices, the habits and the passions that will rule a man's life, Tocqueville said, we must watch the baby in his mother's arms; we must see the first images that the world casts upon the mirror of his mind; we must hear the first words that awaken his sleeping powers of thought. "The entire man," he wrote, "is, so to speak, to be seen in the cradle of the child."

That is why these books on the childhoods of the American presidents are so much to the point. And, as our history shows, a great variety of childhoods can lead to the White House. The record confirms the ancient adage that every American boy, no matter how unpromising his beginnings, can aspire to the presidency. Soon, one hopes, the adage will be extended to include every American girl.

All our presidents thus far have been white males who, within the limits of their gender, reflect the diversity of American life. They were born in nineteen of our states; eight of the last thirteen presidents were born west of the Mississippi. Of all our presidents, Abraham Lincoln had the least promising childhood, yet he became our greatest presi-

Introduction

dent. Oddly enough, presidents who are children of privilege sometimes feel an obligation to reform society in order to give children of poverty a better break. And, with Lincoln the great exception, presidents who are children of poverty sometimes feel that there is no need to reform a society that has enabled them to rise from privation to the summit.

Does schooling make a difference? Harry S. Truman, the only twentieth-century president never to attend college, is generally accounted a near-great president. Actually nine—more than one fifth—of our presidents never went to college at all, including such luminaries as George Washington, Andrew Jackson and Grover Cleveland. But, Truman aside, all the non-college men held the highest office before the twentieth century, and, given the increasing complexity of life, a college education will unquestionably be a necessity in the twenty-first century.

Every reader of this book, girls included, has a right to aspire to the presidency. As you survey the childhoods of those who made it, try to figure out the qualities that brought them to the White House. I would suggest that among those qualities are ambition, determination, discipline, education—and luck.

—ARTHUR M. SCHLESINGER, JR.

Emanuel Leutze's *Washington Crossing the Delaware* is one of the most famous images of the American Revolution, but many of its details are historically inaccurate. Among them: the inclusion of James Monroe, the officer holding the flag. Monroe actually crossed the Delaware River the day before the main body of Washington's troops.

Times that Try Men's Souls

The Third Virginia Regiment limped south through New Jersey along with some 3,000 other troops in the Continental army. The Continental soldiers, under the leadership of General George Washington, had recently been chased from New York by the British. It was December 1776—just six months after the Continental Congress adopted the Declaration of Independence in Philadelphia. Now, with Washington's troops in full retreat, it appeared that the *colonists'* dream of independence from Great Britain would soon end.

Still, fighting spirit remained high in the ranks of the Third Virginia. Unlike many of the other regiments that made up the Continental army, the Third Virginia had been together for nearly a year. The Third Virginia was a rifle regiment, and its members prided themselves on their keen eyes and ability to hit their targets. The 600 soldiers of the Third Virginia had fought valiantly in the Battle of New York, meeting a force of 1,500 redcoats—as British soldiers were called—head-on in an area between the Harlem and Hudson Rivers known as Harlem Heights. Although greatly outnumbered, the

10 | James Monroe

Many American units of the Revolutionary War, including James Monroe's Third Virginia Regiment, weren't nearly as well outfitted as this Continental soldier. But, as the British would discover, the ragtag Americans were a determined foe.

Virginians had held their ground until reinforcements arrived and drove the British off. Harlem Heights was one of the few *skirmishes* won by the colonists in the Battle of New York. It proved that Americans could outfight the British on the field of battle.

And yet, there was no question that the Continental army had failed to live up to Washington's expectations. Other American regiments had run from the fight, much to the general's dismay. From New York, Washington split his troops, sending some north to halt the British advance into upstate New York while taking others south with him to throw a blockade in front of the redcoats in New Jersey.

But Washington's troops had failed to stop the British in New Jersey. Now, the Continental army was in retreat again, heading further south and then across the Delaware River to make camp in Pennsylvania. One of the soldiers trudging south with the Third Virginia Regiment was a young lieutenant named James Monroe. Although he had just turned 18, James was a valued leader in the regiment. He'd acted bravely at Harlem Heights, helping hold the regiment together after two officers, Major Andrew Leitch and Colonel Thomas Knowlton, had been killed in battle.

James Monroe later wrote about that march into Pennsylvania. In particular, he revealed how he continued to be inspired by the gallant figure of George Washington leading the ragtag yet brave Continental army:

> I saw him in my earliest youth in the retreat through Jersey at the head of a small band, or rather, in its rear, for he was always near the enemy, and his countenance and manner made an impression on me which time can never efface. A lieutenant then in the Third Virginia Regiment, I happened to be on guard at Newark, and I counted the force under his immediate command by *platoons* as it passed me, which amounted to less than 3,000 men. A deportment so firm, so dignified, so exalted, but yet so modest and composed, I have never seen in any other person.

Camped along the Delaware River, the Third Virginia Regiment was hardly in a condition to fight again. Since skirmishing with the British in New Jersey, some 400 members of the regiment had been wounded or fallen ill in the icy winter conditions. Of the 17 officers in the Third Virginia, just 5 of them, including Lieutenant Monroe, were considered fit for duty. There was barely enough food for the troops, and their thin uniforms provided little warmth.

While Washington's weary men shivered on the Pennsylvania side of the river, the British troops were enjoying far better conditions along the New Jersey side. Living in comfortable camps or taking over inns and private homes, the redcoats were warm, well fed, and willing to wait out the winter before resuming the fight.

Washington learned that a *garrison* of 3,000 Hessian troops was camped near Trenton, New Jersey. The Hessians were German soldiers hired by the British government to fight against the colonists. Such soldiers, who fight for pay alone, are known as mercenaries.

Washington hatched a plan to stage a surprise attack on the Hessian soldiers. On Christmas Eve, he sent a group of 50 scouts across the Delaware River to spy on the Hessian camp. The scouts were led by Captain William Washington, a distant relative of the general. Captain Washington selected James Monroe as his second in command.

The scouts crossed the Delaware 10 miles north of Trenton in wooden rowboats. Then they made their way south on foot, staying close to the river. James led the first platoon. It was a bitterly cold night. What's more, the scouts had to trudge through a driving storm of sleet and snow.

While heading south toward Trenton, James's platoon aroused some guard dogs outside the home of a doctor named Riker. When the doctor investigated the commotion, he assumed the soldiers were British and demanded they leave his property. James stepped forward and identified the scouts as Americans. Dr. Riker immediately apologized, then gave the men food and drink. He even agreed to accompany them on the march to Trenton, offering his services as surgeon if the need arose.

When James and the scouts approached Trenton, they

Times that Try Men's Souls 13

"A deportment so firm, so dignified, so exalted, but yet so modest and composed, I have never seen in any other person," James Monroe would recall of his fellow Virginian George Washington during the Continental army's retreat through New Jersey in 1776.

thought their eyes were deceiving them. Because of the harsh weather, the Hessians had decided not to post *sentries*. What's more, James found the Hessians already very much in the holiday spirit. The Hessian soldiers were celebrating Christmas by drinking and eating heavily. Quickly, James sent men to return to Washington's camp to inform the general that he would find the Hessian soldiers in no condition for battle.

Back in Pennsylvania, Washington decided to stage the attack without delay. As evening fell on Christmas, he assembled some 2,400 troops on the banks of the Delaware River and prepared to board wooden boats for the crossing. Washington found inspiration for his bold plan in the words of the patriotic writer Thomas Paine, author of the essay "An American Crisis."

14 James Monroe

"These are the times that try men's souls," writer Thomas Paine (at left) declared during the bleak early days of the American Revolution. Paine would have approved of James Monroe, who demonstrated that he was no "sunshine patriot" by serving his country when the cause of independence seemed doomed to failure.

"These are the times that try men's souls," Paine wrote. "The summer soldier and the sunshine patriot will, in this crisis, shrink from the service of his country; but he that stands it now deserves the love and thanks of men and women."

It took all night to get the entire army across the river. Once on the Jersey side, the soldiers marched quickly toward Trenton in a swirling snowstorm. By dawn, the main force of Washington's troops was within a half-mile of the town. That's where they met up with Captain Washington, Lieutenant Monroe, and the other scouts. They marched on.

The Hessians failed to notice Washington's army until the Continentals had reached the first streets of the town. On King Street in Trenton, the Americans found a group of German soldiers attempting to load two cannons. They clearly intended

Times that Try Men's Souls   15

to use the firepower to block the road into town. It was vital that the cannons be taken out of action. Captain Washington and Lieutenant Monroe quickly decided to lead a charge to accomplish this. It would be a dangerous maneuver—the officers and their men would be facing heavy gunfire from Hessian troops protecting the cannons—but it had to be done, and fast.

The two officers drew their swords and led their men on the charge. Guns blasted away as the two sides collided. The Americans soon overwhelmed the Hessians and took the cannons, thus opening the road for the Continental army's advance into Trenton.

"If the enemy had got his *artillery* into operation in a narrow street, it might have checked our movement and given him time to reform and reflect," wrote Major James Wilkinson, who participated in the battle. "We in turn might have been compelled to retreat, which would have been fatal to us."

The troops under George Washington would go on that day to score an important victory. The Battle of Trenton represented a turning point in the American Revolution, giving the colonists hope that they could defeat European armies on the battlefield.

As for James Monroe, he was wounded in the charge that took out the Hessians' cannons on King Street. As James rushed the heavy guns, he was hit in the shoulder by a musket ball. The wound

> **After recovering from his gunshot wound, James Monroe never again saw Dr. Riker. As president, he sought out the doctor's family members to reward them with jobs in his administration, but he was never able to locate them.**

caused heavy bleeding, and James would certainly have died had it not been for the efforts of Dr. Riker, who was at the young lieutenant's side when he was struck down. The doctor stopped the bleeding and bandaged James's injured shoulder. Later, James was carried back across the Delaware River, where he found shelter in the home of Henry Wyncoop. He remained with the Wyncoop family for three months while recovering from the shoulder wound. Because the musket ball had lodged high in James's shoulder near his neck, doctors advised against the risky surgery that would be necessary to remove it. For the rest of his life James Monroe carried the musket ball in his shoulder, a souvenir of his brave action on a critical day in American history.

The events around Christmas 1776 have become familiar to generations of Americans since, but over the years a healthy dose of myth has been mixed into the story. Interestingly, the most recognizable image of the American triumph was created not by an eyewitness to the events but by a German immigrant who wasn't even born until 40 years after the Continental army had routed the Hessians at Trenton. In 1851, Emanuel Leutze painted *Washington Crossing the Delaware*. The painting, which hangs in the Metropolitan Museum of Art in New York, has been seen by millions of Americans. It depicts a gallant George Washington standing steadfast in a boat

> During James Monroe's presidency, Congress passed legislation permanently fixing the number of red and white stripes on the American flag at 13 in honor of the 13 original colonies.

while a group of hardy sailors rows the vessel through the icy waters of the Delaware River.

Historians agree that Emanuel Leutze's depiction of Washington and his men bears little resemblance to the truth. For example, the painting shows Washington making the crossing during daylight. The actual crossing occurred at night. What's more, it is highly unlikely that the general would have been standing in the boat. Why would he have risked falling into the icy waters? In reality, Washington probably sat in the rear of the boat, huddled under heavy cloaks and blankets to take cover from the cold.

> In 1820, James Monroe was reelected with all but one vote cast in the electoral college. New Hampshire governor William Plumer cast the single vote against Monroe, explaining that he believed George Washington should be the only president ever elected unanimously.

Finally, the Leutze painting shows a young army officer holding the American flag behind Washington. That officer is supposed to be Lieutenant James Monroe. Of course, it is well known that Monroe crossed the Delaware River the night before, so he couldn't possibly have shared a boat with General Washington.

Despite these historical inaccuracies, Leutze did capture the drama of the American Revolution in *Washington Crossing the Delaware*. And the fact that he chose to include the images of two men who went on to become president of the United States certainly enhances the patriotic spirit of the painting. One of those future presidents was, of course, George Washington. The other was James Monroe.

Westmoreland County

Westmoreland County sits on a wide finger of land in Virginia bordered on the north by the Potomac River and the south by the Rappahannock River. While the citizens of most counties would be delighted if they could claim a single president of the United States, the people of Westmoreland County can say that two of America's greatest presidents have ties to their county. In addition to James Monroe, George Washington—who one day would be Monroe's commander during the American Revolution—was also born in Westmoreland County. During their childhoods, the county was mostly a land of farms and *plantations*. Monroe and Washington spent their youths as farm boys in Westmoreland, learning how to till the soil and raise crops.

Westmoreland County was also the home of the famous Lee family. Two members of the family, Richard Henry Lee and Francis Lightfoot Lee, were signers of the Declaration of

Popes Creek in Westmoreland County, Virginia. James Monroe's family ties to the county—which has produced two American presidents—stretched back to 1650.

Independence. Another member of the family, Henry Lee, had a distinguished military career, serving under Washington during the American Revolution and then winning election to Congress. His son, Robert E. Lee, would lead the Confederate army during the Civil War.

John Marshall was another boy with ties to Westmoreland County. Marshall, who attended school in Westmoreland, was a classmate and friend of James Monroe. Later, he would become one of America's brightest legal scholars and win appointment as chief justice of the United States.

It might be argued, then, that no place in America contributed more to the early development of the nation than did Westmoreland County.

James Monroe's family ties to the county stretched back to 1650. In that year, his ancestor Andrew Monroe left Scotland and immigrated to Virginia. When Andrew Monroe arrived, Virginia was still very much wild and unexplored country. Just 43 years before, the first permanent settlement in America had been founded not far from Westmoreland County in Jamestown. Despite the harsh winters, unpredictable harvests, and hostile Indians, Monroe established a plantation with a comfortable estate home he named Monroe Hall. He took the liberty of naming a nearby stream Monroe Creek. The creek is a *tributary* of the Potomac River.

Andrew Monroe died in 1668. Monroe Hall and the surrounding plantation were passed down through the generations. Eventually Spence Monroe inherited the estate. Spence Monroe married Elizabeth Jones, and on April 28, 1758, their oldest son, James, was born. James's older sister, Elizabeth,

Slaves worked the small Virginia plantation of James Monroe's boyhood, but as an adult Monroe would come to regard slavery as wrong.

had been born four years earlier. Two younger brothers would follow James.

Spence and Elizabeth Monroe were hardworking Virginians, but they were hardly wealthy. At the time of James's birth, the Monroe plantation included just 500 acres, which was not considered large in the colonial era. In contrast, the plantation owned by the Washington family sprawled over some 6,000 acres.

The Monroes grew tobacco, corn, and barley. They also raised cattle. Still, the Monroes found they could not live only from the profits of the plantation. And so Spence Monroe practiced a trade: cabinetmaking. Using just the simplest hand tools—there were no power saws or electric drills in colonial days—Spence Monroe fashioned chairs, tables, cupboards, and other pieces of furniture from the trees he cut down in the Westmoreland countryside. He also whittled toys for his children out of tree limbs and other small pieces of wood.

The Monroes owned slaves, which was certainly not unusual in colonial Virginia. Spence Monroe was known to have owned a slave named Muddy, who learned the craft of cabinetmaking and assisted James Monroe's father in his shop.

As a child growing up in colonial Virginia, James Monroe learned how to use a gun. James owned a flintlock, which was given to him by his father when he was six years old. Flint, a rough stone, was used to trigger the gunpowder packed into the gun's barrel. When the shooter squeezed the trigger of the flintlock, the flint stone would strike against a piece of steel,

James Monroe developed into an excellent marksman through years of hunting ducks and geese. His father had given him his first flintlock when James was six.

creating a spark. The spark would then ignite the gunpowder, causing a small explosion, which would propel the bullet. Gunpowder was loaded into the gun through the muzzle, which is the mouth at the end of the barrel. It was then packed down hard with a long iron rod known as a ramrod.

James used his flintlock for "fowling," meaning he hunted birds with the weapon. On fowling trips into the Westmoreland County marshes to bag wild birds such as geese and ducks for his family's supper table, James developed his keen aim. That skill would later serve him well as an officer in the Third Virginia Regiment.

It's likely that James Monroe would have followed his father into farming and cabinetmaking. The Monroes weren't wealthy enough to afford educations for their children at William and Mary College, which at the time was the finest school in the Virginia colony. As such, a career in law, teaching, or another profession seemed out of the question for the boy. What's more, in colonial days, it was not unusual for the eldest son to take up the trade of the father.

But in 1774, when James was 16 years old, Spence Monroe died. At the time, James was enrolled as a day student at Campbelltown Academy, a private school in Westmoreland County led by the Reverend Archibald Campbell, head of a local Protestant church. It was at Campbelltown that James became friendly with fellow student John Marshall. Campbell made sure his students were drilled in mathematics and Latin, the ancient language of the Romans. By the 1700s few

James Monroe was the first president to ride in a steamboat.

> During his career in public service James Monroe earned a reputation for honesty. Thomas Jefferson said, "Monroe was so honest that if you turned his soul inside out there would not be a spot on it."

people spoke Latin fluently, but it was still employed in religious services, and many of its terms were used in the education of doctors and lawyers. Under Campbell's guidance, James became a fluent speaker of Latin.

In the colonial era it was customary for the oldest son to inherit the wealth of the family. In turn, he was expected to provide for the education of the other children and to make sure they received help establishing businesses or trades. At the time of Spence Monroe's death, the other children were sons Andrew and Joseph and daughter Elizabeth. But the task of caring for the Monroe plantation and seeing to the needs of his brothers and sister was too great a burden for the 16-year-old James. So James's uncle Joseph Jones stepped in and took over many of the responsibilities of the Monroe family.

Educated as an attorney, Joseph Jones had been a member of the Virginia House of Burgesses, representing neighboring King George County. The House of Burgesses was the oldest established *legislature* in the colonies. It was the first attempt by colonists in America to govern themselves and make their own laws. Following the American Revolution, Jones would serve on the Virginia Supreme Court and would become a friend and counselor to Washington, Jefferson, Madison, and, of course, his nephew James Monroe.

> The United States Marine Corps Band played at James Monroe's inauguration in 1821 and since then has never missed a presidential inauguration.

Westmoreland County 25

Virginia has produced more presidents than any other state, and two of them—George Washington and James Monroe—were born in Westmoreland County, between the Potomac and Rappahannock Rivers.

At the time of Spence Monroe's death, Joseph Jones had no *heirs* of his own. He was fond of his nephew James and concluded that the boy was much too bright to spend his days in the tobacco fields. So he decided to provide for the boy's education, taking it upon himself to pay the *tuition* for James to attend William and Mary College.

The Wren Building, where James Monroe lived while he was a student at William and Mary College in Williamsburg, Virginia, from 1774 to 1776.

William and Mary

The College of William and Mary, founded in the colony of Virginia in 1693, has the distinction of being America's second-oldest college. (The oldest is Harvard, which was established in 1636.) William and Mary has produced a handful of American presidents, including Thomas Jefferson, John Tyler, and James Monroe.

The College of William and Mary was named for King William II and Queen Mary of England, under whom it was granted a *charter* to open. In 1774, when James Monroe walked onto the William and Mary campus in Williamsburg for the first time, he found a bustling school much larger than the tiny private academy run by the Reverend Archibald Campbell, who limited his class size to 25.

James, 16 when he entered college, moved into the Sir Christopher Wren Building, named for the famed British architect who designed it. His roommate in the *dormitory* was John Francis Mercer, the 15-year-old son of a wealthy plantation owner in Stafford County, Virginia. James and Mercer would become close personal friends, and in a short time both young men would enlist in the Third Virginia Regiment.

Another student at William and Mary was John Marshall, James's friend from Campbelltown Academy.

At the college, James Monroe studied Latin and law. His law professor was George Wythe, one of the most famous lawyers in the colonies. For James and his classmates, it was an exciting time to be away from home and on their own. Everywhere in the colonies, people were agitating for independence from Great Britain. As a student, James studied the law set down by King George and knew it was unfair. The colonists, James believed, should have the right to govern themselves and write their own laws.

> **The Wren Building remains standing on the William and Mary campus. Over the years the Wren Building has burned down and been rebuilt three times. It is no longer used as a dormitory, although students still attend classes in the facility.**

Life wasn't always so serious on campus, though. At William and Mary, James Monroe befriended James Innes, a 20-year-old student who was regarded as a troublemaker by the faculty. In the spring of 1775, just a few months after James Monroe started his studies at William and Mary, Innes circulated a *petition* complaining about the quality of food served to the students by Maria Diggs. As "mistress of the college," Diggs was responsible for feeding the students, cleaning their rooms, and taking care of their laundry. Innes convinced James and several other students to sign the petition, then brought the paper to college authorities.

A hearing was scheduled to investigate the issue. James was asked to testify, but when he spoke about the charges

John Marshall, a friend of James Monroe's from Campbelltown Academy and William and Mary College, would go on to a distinguished legal career. Marshall served as chief justice of the United States from 1801 to 1835.

against Maria Diggs he admitted that he didn't agree with them. What's more, he said, he hadn't even read the petition but had signed it simply because his friend Innes asked him to. Maria Diggs was found innocent of the charge of feeding bland food to the William and Mary students, and James Innes was punished for bringing the false charges. A few months later, in the summer of 1775, the faculty breathed a sigh of relief when Innes withdrew from the college and took his mischievous ways with him.

But the students at William and Mary continued to look up to James Innes. The opening shots in the colonists' war with England had been fired, and the campus troublemaker had left college to join the fight.

James Monroe ached to go with him.

4

Reenactment of a session of the House of Burgesses. When James Monroe arrived in Williamsburg in 1774, tension between the legislative body and Virginia's royal governor was approaching the boiling point.

Williamsburg

When James Monroe arrived in the Virginia capital of Williamsburg to begin classes at William and Mary, he witnessed a dramatic and history-making event in the House of Burgesses, the colony's legislature. By the summer of 1774, some colonists throughout America had begun talking about independence from England. King George, fearing that this talk could lead to revolution, took steps to silence people opposed to British rule. In Virginia, he ordered the House of Burgesses dissolved. He directed the royal governor, Lord Dunmore, to carry out his wishes.

But the burgesses refused to comply with the governor's order. Instead, members of the legislature met at the Raleigh Tavern in Williamsburg in defiance of Dunmore and the king.

Dunmore endured the defiance of the burgesses for a while. But in the spring of 1775, he decided to take action to prevent the Virginia colonists from starting an armed uprising. In the center of Williamsburg stood a small warehouse where gunpowder was stored. Dunmore dispatched a regiment of British troops to seize the gunpowder. News of the seizure spread throughout Virginia. Colonial leaders decided it was time to call up town *militias* to march on Williamsburg for a confrontation with British troops. One of the largest militias to answer the call was led by a patriot named Patrick Henry. As Henry's troops neared Williamsburg, he was met by a representative of the governor, who offered to pay for the seized powder. Henry accepted the *compromise* to avoid bloodshed, and tempers eased.

Many young people attending class on the William and Mary campus watched these events unfold and resolved to become involved. James Innes organized a military unit among the students. The former class clown drilled his recruits on the Palace Green, a park in Williamsburg. James Monroe was an eager participant.

By now, James had grown into a leader. Physically he presented a commanding appearance. Standing just over six feet tall, he was lean but powerfully built, with broad shoulders and well-muscled arms developed during his younger years working on the Monroe family plantation. Though quiet, he was by no means shy. He had earned the respect of the other students because he was never the type to act without giving careful thought to his options. Later, as president, James Monroe would be regarded as one of the most intelligent men to serve in the office.

The burgesses returned to Williamsburg in the summer of 1775. By now, fervor for revolution had swept throughout the colonies. Earlier that year, colonists in the Massachusetts towns of Lexington and Concord had skirmished with British troops. When Virginia's colonial leaders met that summer in Williamsburg, it would be the last time the legislators gath-

Williamsburg 33

King George III's efforts to stifle dissent in the American colonies only fanned the flames of rebellion.

ered under the authority of the king. At their sessions that summer the burgesses made it clear that they no longer regarded themselves as subjects of King George. Knowing that a full-blown war was now inevitable, Governor Dunmore fled Williamsburg.

On June 24, James Monroe, now just 17 years old, joined 23 other William and Mary students in a raid on Dunmore's mansion. With the governor and his bodyguards already gone, the William and Mary students encountered no resistance. They seized some 200 muskets, 300 swords, and assorted other weapons and turned them over to the Williamsburg militia.

In the spring of 1776, the Continental Congress convened in Philadelphia. Among other business, Congress issued an

34 James Monroe

A view of the governor's mansion in Williamsburg. On June 24, 1775, James Monroe was among a group of two dozen William and Mary students who raided the mansion. Encountering no resistance, the students seized a cache of weapons.

order that "six companies of expert riflemen be immediately raised in Pennsylvania, two in Maryland and two in Virginia."

James Monroe and his roommate, John Mercer, decided they could no longer remain out of the fray. The two young men withdrew from William and Mary and enlisted in the Third Virginia Regiment. Within weeks, both had been promoted to the rank of lieutenant.

Little about the Third Virginia made it look like an army. The only uniforms issued to the Virginians were fringed buck-

Patrick Henry (at right), a firebrand who had declared, "Give me liberty or give me death," was placed in charge of all of Virginia's troops in 1776. Eighteen-year-old James Monroe joined the Third Virginia Regiment, which was commanded by Colonel Hugh Mercer, a good friend of Monroe's uncle Joseph Jones.

skin shirts and *tricorn* hats, which the men were ordered to wear cocked to one side.

The Third Virginia trained hard that spring and summer. By midsummer, the Virginians were preparing to march north to New York to join the Continental army under the leadership of General George Washington. Just a few weeks before, in Philadelphia, delegates to the Continental Congress had adopted the Declaration of Independence.

On a morning in early August of 1776, Lieutenant James Monroe shouldered his rifle and fell in step with the 600 men of the Third Virginia Regiment. James, now 18 years old, was leaving his home to fight for the cause of independence.

James Monroe, fifth president of the United States, presided over a time of peace and prosperity that came to be known as the Era of Good Feelings.

The Era of Good Feelings

After recovering from the wound he suffered at the Battle of Trenton, James Monroe rejoined the Continental army. He fought in the Battle of Brandywine, spent the winter of 1777–78 at Valley Forge, then resigned from the army in 1778 at the rank of lieutenant colonel. He intended to raise his own fighting unit, but that plan failed, and he remained a civilian through the end of the war.

Back in Virginia he befriended Governor Thomas Jefferson, who urged James to return to his law studies. James followed Jefferson's advice, but while studying for a career in law he received a grant of 5,600 acres of land in Virginia in payment for his service during the Revolution. This made him one of his state's major landowners and wealthiest citizens.

James abandoned his plans for a law career, but he didn't just want to be a gentleman farmer, either. Instead, he won election to the Virginia House of Delegates, his state's legislature. In 1783 he became a member of the Continental Congress. He was one of the first American lawmakers to urge his nation to push its borders westward. In fact, James Monroe himself bought some 50,000 acres of land in the wilderness of

Kentucky. During 1783 and 1784 he spent months traveling in the frontier, writing, "In this trip I shall take, I may perhaps acquire a better knowledge of the posts [where] we [should] Occupy . . . the temper of the Indians [toward] us, as well as the soil, water's and in [general] the natural view of the country."

In the fall of 1784, James Monroe returned to Congress, which at that time was meeting in New York City. There he met a beautiful young New York *socialite* named Elizabeth Kortright. The couple married in 1786 and would raise two daughters: Eliza and Maria Hester. A son, James Spence, died in infancy. The Monroes established a home on a Virginia plantation known as Highland.

James Monroe wouldn't spend much time at home, though. He was elected to the U.S. Senate in 1790 and appointed minister to France in 1794. He returned home and in 1799 was elected governor of Virginia, a post he held until 1802. From 1803 until 1807 he served in diplomatic roles in France, Spain, and England. As President Thomas Jefferson's representative in France, he headed the negotiations with the government of Napoleon Bonaparte to obtain the Louisiana Purchase, which added some 800,000 square miles to the United States.

In 1811, with a second war against England looming, Monroe was appointed secretary of state by President James Madison, his friend and fellow Virginian. He served as Madison's chief diplomat during the War of 1812 and later served as secretary of war as well.

James Monroe was himself elected president in 1816 and reelected in 1820. He presided over a time of peace and pros-

A mid-19th-century view of Monrovia. Liberia's capital city was named in honor of President Monroe, a strong supporter of establishing a colony for freed black slaves in West Africa.

perity in American life known as the Era of Good Feelings. During his presidency pioneers opened the so-called Cumberland Road, a route that enabled travelers to ride overland as far west as Wheeling in western Virginia. Meanwhile, the country continued to grow. By the time Monroe left office, 24 states had been admitted to the Union and western trails were opened all the way to the Pacific Ocean.

Nevertheless, the Era of Good Feelings was perhaps a much too rosy description of the times, because many troubles arose during the Monroe presidency. Some of the states that entered the Union at this time permitted slavery, which troubled *abolitionists* in the North. In 1820, President Monroe signed a bill known as the Missouri Compromise. It permitted Missouri, a slave state, to enter the Union along with Maine, a free state. The Missouri Compromise also banned slavery in

40   James Monroe

This illustration depicts James Monroe (standing before the globe) and his advisers as they craft the Monroe Doctrine. The most significant achievement of President Monroe's administration, the doctrine declared that the United States wouldn't tolerate further European interference in the Western Hemisphere.

states and territories north and west of Missouri.

Although he had grown up in a slave state, Monroe knew that slavery was wrong and would not last in America. As president, he supported the establishment of the American Colonization Society, which helped found the nation of Liberia in Africa as a home for freed blacks. The capital of Liberia was named Monrovia in his honor.

During James Monroe's presidency, America acquired Florida from Spain—but not through the gentlemanly art of diplomacy. President Monroe had dispatched General

The Era of Good Feelings

Andrew Jackson to drive the Seminole Indians, who were attacking white settlements, out of Georgia. Jackson's troops not only chased the Indians out of Georgia, but also pursued them into Florida, where they burned Indian villages and hanged tribal leaders. With Jackson's army firmly in control of Florida, President Monroe's secretary of state, John Quincy Adams, demanded that Spain sell the territory to America for $5 million. Though opposed to the deal, the Spanish reluctantly agreed, not wishing to risk war with the United States.

Success in getting Spain to give up Florida set the stage for President Monroe's most important policy: the Monroe Doctrine. In 1823, the president delivered a speech in which he warned European nations against further interference in the Western *Hemisphere*. "The American continents," he declared, "by the free and independent condition which they have assumed and maintain, are henceforth not to be considered as subjects for future colonization by any European power."

The Monroe Doctrine served notice on Europe that America intended to dominate its own corner of the globe. This, it might be argued, put the United States on the path to becoming a world power.

After leaving the White House in 1825, James and Elizabeth Monroe retired to their Virginia plantation. Elizabeth Monroe died on September 23, 1830. James Monroe died at the New York City home of his daughter Maria Hester. The date of the fifth president's death was July 4, 1831—Independence Day—exactly five years after the deaths of the second and third presidents, John Adams and Thomas Jefferson.

Chronology

1758 James Monroe born in Westmoreland County, Virginia.

1774 Enters the College of William and Mary.

1776 Enlists in the Third Virginia Regiment; wounded at the Battle of Trenton while leading a charge to capture Hessian cannons.

1782 Elected to the Virginia House of Delegates.

1786 Marries Elizabeth Kortright.

1790 Elected to U.S. Senate.

1794 Appointed minister to France.

1799 Elected governor of Virginia.

1811 Serves as secretary of state.

1814 Appointed secretary of war.

1816 Elected president.

1820 Reelected president; signs Missouri Compromise, outlawing slavery north and west of Missouri.

1823 Issues Monroe Doctrine, barring European colonization in the Western Hemisphere.

1825 Leaves office.

1831 Dies in New York City.

Glossary

abolitionist—an American who called for an end to slavery before or during the Civil War.

artillery—large guns, such as cannons, used by a military force.

charter—a grant of rights or privileges from a government.

colonists—people who settle in a new land and form a community.

compromise—an agreement between two parties to settle their differences by giving both parties some, but not all, of what they want.

dormitory—a building at a school or college where students reside.

garrison—a usually permanent military post, or the soldiers stationed there.

heir—someone who inherits money or other property upon the death of a relative or other person.

hemisphere—half of the earth.

legislature—the governing body of a state, composed of representatives elected by the people.

militia—a fighting force of volunteers, usually formed by a state or local government.

petition—a formal request, usually signed by several people, made to a government or other authority for a specific purpose.

plantation—a large farm that grows tobacco, coffee, cotton, and similar crops.

platoon—a small military unit, usually made up of two or more squads of soldiers.

sentries—soldiers posted to guard military camps.

skirmish—a minor fight between enemy forces, often as part of a larger war.

socialite—a socially active, well-known, and frequently wealthy person.

tributary—a small stream that flows into a larger waterway, such as a river or lake.

tricorn—a three-cornered hat common in colonial days.

tuition—a fee charged students to attend a school or college.

Further Reading

Ammon, Harry. *James Monroe: The Quest for National Identity*. New York: McGraw-Hill, 1971.

Brown, Stuart Gerry, ed. *The Autobiography of James Monroe*. Syracuse, N.Y.: Syracuse University Press, 1959.

Dwyer, William M. *The Day Is Ours: How a Ragged Rebel Army Stood the Storm and Saved the Revolution*. New York: Viking Press, 1983.

Hanser, Richard. *The Glorious Hour of Lt. Monroe*. New York: Atheneum, 1976.

Hutton, Ann Hawkes. *George Washington Crossed Here*. Philadelphia: Franklin Publishing Co., 1966.

Langston-Harrison, Lee. *A Presidential Legacy: The Monroe Collection*. Fredericksburg, Va.: James Monroe Museum and Memorial Library, 1997.

Internet Resources

- http://monticello.avenue.org/ashlawn/
    Ash Lawn-Highland, home of James and Elizabeth Monroe

- http://www.westmoreland-county.org
    Westmoreland County, Virginia

- http://www.whitehouse.gov/history/presidents/jm5.html
    The White House Biography of James Monroe

- http://www.whitehouse.gov/history/firstladies/em5.html
    The White House Biography of Elizabeth Kortright Monroe

- http://www.wm.edu
    William and Mary College

Index

Adams, John, 41
Adams, John Quincy, 41
American Colonization Society, 40
American Revolution, 15, 17, 20, 25, 33–35, 37

Brandywine Creek, battle of, 37

Campbell, Archibald, 24, 27
Campbelltown Academy, 24, 28
College of William and Mary, 23, 25, 27–29, 31, 32, 33, 34
Continental army, 9, 10, 35, 37
Continental Congress, 9, 33, 35, 37

Declaration of Independence, 9, 35
Delaware River, 10, 11, 12, 13, 16, 17
Diggs, Maria, 28, 29

Era of Good Feelings, the, 38–41

George III, king of Great Britain, 28, 31, 32
Great Britain, 9, 10, 12, 28, 31, 32, 34, 35

Harlem Heights, battle of, 9, 10, 11
Henry, Patrick, 32
Hessians, 12, 13, 14, 15
Highland plantation, 38, 41

Innes, James, 28, 29, 32

Jackson, Andrew, 41
Jamestown, 20
Jefferson, Thomas, 25, 27, 37, 38, 41
Jones, Joseph (uncle), 24–25

Knowlton, Thomas, 11

Lee, Francis Lightfoot, 20

Lee, Henry, 20
Lee, Richard Henry, 20
Lee, Robert E., 20
Leitch, Andrew, 11
Leutze, Emanuel, 16, 17
Lexington and Concord, battle of, 32
Liberia, 40

Madison, James, 25, 38
Marshall, John, 20, 24, 28
Mary, queen of England, 27
Maryland, 34
Mercer, John Francis, 27, 34
Missouri Compromise, 39–40
Monroe, Andrew (brother), 21, 24
Monroe, Andrew (ancestor), 20
Monroe, Eliza (daughter), 38
Monroe, Elizabeth (sister), 21, 24
Monroe, Elizabeth Jones (mother), 21
Monroe, Elizabeth Kortright (wife), 38, 41
Monroe, James
  ancestry of, 20–21
  birth of, 19, 21
  education of, 23, 24, 25, 27–29, 31, 32, 33, 34, 37
  and death of father, 23, 24–25
  and plantation life, 19, 21–22,
  political career of, 37–41
  and slavery, 22, 39–40
  with Third Virginia Regiment during the American Revolution, 11–16, 17, 23, 27–28, 32, 33, 34–35, 37
Monroe, James Spence (son), 38
Monroe, Joseph (brother), 21, 24
Monroe, Maria Hester (daughter), 38, 41
Monroe, Spence (father), 21, 22, 23, 24
Monroe Doctrine, 41

Index

Napoleon Bonaparte, 38
Newark, 11
New Jersey, 10, 11, 14
New York, 9, 10, 16, 35, 38, 41

Paine, Thomas, 13–14
Pennsylvania, 10, 11, 13, 34
Philadelphia, 9, 33, 35
Potomac River, 19, 20

Rappahannock River, 19
Riker, Doctor, 12, 16

Spain, 38, 40, 41

Third Virginia Regiment, 9, 11, 23, 27–28, 34–35
Trenton, battle of, 12, 14, 15, 37
Tyler, John, 27

Valley Forge, 37
Virginia House of Burgesses, 24–25, 31

Washington, George, 9, 10, 11, 12, 13, 14, 16, 17, 19, 20, 21, 25, 35
Washington, William, 12, 14, 15
Washington Crossing the Delaware, 16–17
Westmoreland County, Virginia, 19, 20, 22, 23, 24
William II, king of England, 27
Williamsburg, 27, 31, 32, 33
Wilkinson, James, 15
Wren Building, 27
Wyncoop, Henry, 16
Wythe, George, 28

Picture Credits

3:	Bettmann/Corbis
8:	Art Resource, NY
10:	North Wind Picture Archives
13:	Independence National Historical Park, Philadelphia
14:	Bettmann/Corbis
18:	Lee Snider; Lee Snider/Corbis
21:	Courtesy of the Colonial Williamsburg Foundation
22:	Historical Picture Archive/Corbis
25:	© OTTN Publishing
26:	Courtesy of the Colonial Williamsburg Foundation
29:	Independence National Historical Park, Philadelphia
30:	Courtesy of the Colonial Williamsburg Foundation
33:	Courtesy of the Colonial Williamsburg Foundation
34:	Courtesy of the Colonial Williamsburg Foundation
35:	Courtesy of the Colonial Williamsburg Foundation
36:	Independence National Historical Park, Philadelphia
39:	Corbis
40:	Bettmann/Corbis

Cover photos: (left) Corbis Images; (center, right) Independence National Historical Park, Philadelphia;

Contributors

ARTHUR M. SCHLESINGER JR. holds the Albert Schweitzer Chair in the Humanities at the Graduate Center of the City University of New York. He is the author of more than a dozen books, including *The Age of Jackson*; *The Vital Center*; *The Age of Roosevelt* (3 vols.); *A Thousand Days: John F. Kennedy in the White House*; *Robert Kennedy and His Times*; *The Cycles of American History*; and *The Imperial Presidency*. Professor Schlesinger served as Special Assistant to President Kennedy (1961–63). His numerous awards include the Pulitzer Prize for History; the Pulitzer Prize for Biography; two National Book Awards; the Bancroft Prize; and the American Academy of Arts and Letters Gold Medal for History.

HAL MARCOVITZ is a journalist for *The Morning Call*, a newspaper based in Allentown, Pennsylvania. His other titles in the CHILDHOODS OF THE PRESIDENTS series are *Theodore Roosevelt*, *John F. Kennedy*, *John Adams*, and *Bill Clinton*. He lives in Chalfont, Pennsylvania, with his wife, Gail, and daughters Ashley and Michelle.